T H E
DEACON
I WANT TO BE

MANUAL

JOHNNY HUNT

SAMPSON
RESOURCES

4887 Alpha, Suite 220 • Dallas, Texas 75244 • (972) 387-2806 • (800) 371-5248 • FAX 972-387-0150
www.sampsonresources.com   info@sampsonresources.com

HOW TO USE THIS MANUAL

THE DEACON I WANT TO BE manual accompanies the six video lessons by Johnny Hunt. The manual is vital to the study—it helps make practical application of Dr. Hunt's video lessons and is a reference to which you can refer for years to come. Use it aggressively! Whether you are completing the study with a group of men or on your own, be sure to take notes on the video lessons and then work through the discussion guide, writing down your thoughts, ideas, and comments. Fill in every blank. NOTE: Each lesson — video and discussion — is designed to be completed in one to one and one half hours, but if you are unable to finish in the allotted time, feel free to continue it in the next session or complete the lessons on your own. May God bless you in your study of THE DEACON I WANT TO BE.

TABLE OF CONTENTS

1

THE DEACON AND HIS WORTHINESS

His Qualifications, His Calling and His Walk with Christ

INTRODUCTION

As a pastor, I can assure you that there's nothing better than walking into a deacons meeting knowing in your heart that your deacons are qualified, work together in harmony, enjoy one another, and take their calling seriously. It just doesn't get any better than that!

In Ephesians 4:1-2, Paul tells believers how to "walk worthy of the calling" God has placed on their life. Though these instructions are given to every believer in the entire church body, they apply especially to deacons. Note Paul's words.

> *I, therefore, the prisoner of the Lord, beseech you to walk worthy of the calling with which you were called, with all lowliness and gentleness, with longsuffering, bearing with one another in love…* (Ephesians 4:1-2)

Since our study specifically relates to deacons, here are five characteristics from this passage that clearly demonstrate how deacons *walk worthy* of their calling:

- By knowing that they have been *called by God* to serve
- By being *faithful* in their service
- By humbly viewing service as a *privilege*, not as a *right*
- By exercising *patience* as they serve
- By exemplifying a *forgiving* spirit

While these five characteristics show all believers—including deacons—how to walk worthy of their calling, the Bible goes further by listing qualifications that apply specifically to deacons. As we will see, much focus is placed on the deacon's *character*. The church, therefore, should select deacons only after examining their *character*, *conduct* and *commitment* to the Lord.

SETTING

As an apostle and pastor, Paul was sent by God to plant churches from Judea all the way to Rome. So naturally, he had a profound love for the churches he began. When he wrote to Timothy, he did so as a loving pastor. Since Paul knew his time on this earth was drawing to a close, he was particularly concerned that the churches he had poured his heart and soul into would continue on, healthy and stable without him.

Paul first lists the criteria for the pastor (1 Timothy 3:1-7), then follows with a list of qualifications the church is to use for deacons. Here is what he says.

> *Likewise deacons must be reverent, not double-tongued, not given to much wine, not greedy for money, holding the mystery of the faith with a pure conscience. But let these also first be tested; then let them serve as deacons, being found blameless. Likewise, their wives must be reverent,*

not slanderers, temperate, faithful in all things. Let deacons be the husbands of one wife, ruling their children and their own houses well. For those who have served well as deacons obtain for themselves a good standing and great boldness in the faith which is in Christ Jesus. (1 Timothy 3:8-13)

Note that the qualifications Paul outlines for deacons are purposely set against the backdrop of the qualifications for pastors. In addition, the similarities between the qualifications of pastors and deacons underscore the awesome responsibility deacons have for service.

QUALIFICATIONS

Careful examination of the biblical qualifications yields valuable insight about men being considered for ordination as well as deacons being reactivated for service. Let's consider each qualification individually.

1. A deacon must have a good reputation. (1 Timothy 3:8) A wealthy businessman once said: "It takes 20 years to build a reputation and five minutes to ruin it. If you think about that, you'll do things differently." The Bible makes the same claim on a man's reputation: "Don't lose your grip on Love and Loyalty. Tie them around your neck; carve their initials on your heart. Earn a reputation for living well in God's eyes and the eyes of the people." (Proverbs 3:3, *The Message*)

The Bible uses the word "reverent" in the first qualification we consider. Recalling the initial process that called into existence the office of deacon, having a good reputation stood as the first apostolic requirement that the early church observed when men were called and chosen to serve.

Therefore, brethren, seek out from among you seven men of good reputation, full of the Holy Spirit and wisdom, whom we may appoint over this business. (Acts 6:3)

The phrase "of good reputation" is synonymous with the word "reverent." Acts 6:3 brings clarity to the concept of "reverent":

- To be *reverent* is to be "honorable," and being full of wisdom makes one "honorable."

- To be *reverent* is also to be "devout," and being full of the Holy Spirit makes one "devout."

If the men whom we examine are found to be full of the Holy Spirit and wisdom, they will likely become deacons who grow in faith and remain faithful in service. Finally, it should be noted that a deacon's reputation is not limited to the church family alone. His reputation must be stellar outside the church as well as inside the church.

2. A deacon must be a man of his word. (1 Timothy 3:8) To be "double-tongued" means to twist the truth, to relay a story one way to one person and another way another person. Men who twist the truth and are "double-tongued" disqualify themselves to serve as a deacon. If a deacon is a man of his word, his word can be trusted. Someone wrote, "When regard for truth has been broken down or even slightly weakened, all things will remain doubtful." Deacons must not be men of weak, doubtful words. If they are, people will not believe them or trust them—and they certainly will not follow them. A columnist once wrote to an inquirer: "The naked truth is always better than the best dressed lie." No statement could be any clearer. A deacon is a man who can be trusted. He is a man of his word.

3. A deacon must be without offense. (1 Timothy 3:8) If we look back at the first qualification of a deacon (good reputation), and compare that to the activities associated with the use of alcohol in our society today, we must conclude that there is no way that the use of alcohol can enhance the reputation of a deacon. On the other hand, it can do irreparable damage.

The phrase "given to much wine" describes a person who "sits around drinking to excess." The

> The similarities between the qualifications of pastors and deacons underscore the awesome responsibility deacons have for service.

Bible says, "It is good neither to eat meat nor drink wine nor do anything by which your brother stumbles or is offended or is made weak" (Romans 14:21). Drinking inevitably brings offense and stumbling blocks both to the believer and the unbeliever. A deacon must guard at all costs against becoming an offense to others.

4. A deacon must be a generous giver. (1 Timothy 3:8) Ron Blue, a noted Christian businessman and financial expert, says that the only antidote for greed (materialism) is generous giving. The best understanding of "greedy for money" is "an eagerness for dishonest gain." It is not wrong to earn money, spend money, invest money or save money. The danger is being so attached to money that a person is motivated to acquire it dishonestly and use it irresponsibly.

> One of my personal favorite sayings is, "We are never more like Jesus than when we *give*."

A faithful church member from North Carolina was known for saying, "You will never miss anything you give away." One of my personal favorite sayings is, "We are never more like Jesus than when we *give*." The Bible is clear that we cannot love both God and money.

Here's the bottom line: Deacons ought to tithe. If deacons do not tithe, I believe they serve the church with an *absent* heart. The Bible gives us clear warnings about the consequences of being greedy for money, and no deacon serves faithfully who fosters greed in his heart. Effective deacons are always generous givers.

5. A deacon must have a good grip on God's Word. (1 Timothy 3:9) "Holding the mystery of the faith with a pure conscience" suggests having a clear understanding of basic biblical teachings. Every deacon should have a clear understanding of basic Christian doctrines such as salvation by grace through faith, the virgin birth of Christ, the resur-

rection, the doctrine of the church, the rapture, and many others.

In Colossians 3:16, Paul exhorts believers to "Let the Word of Christ dwell in you richly…" If this is expected of *all* believers, how much more should it apply to deacons who are called to serve the church. Observe another passage: "Your Word I have hidden in my heart that I might not sin against you" (Psalm 119:11). If God's Word works as a deterrent in my heart keeping me from sin, then I want as much of it as I can possibly have!

Having a strong grip on God's Word produces two indispensable effects in deacons: 1) they trust in God's promises and 2) they believe in God's power. Trust and belief help deacons maintain proper commitment and capacity to serve the church family. A deacon must not only *know* the Word of God, he must also *do* the Word of God.

6. A deacon must be proven. (1 Timothy 3:10) A man is not ordained as a deacon in order to *acquire* these qualifications. He is ordained because he already *has* them. A prospective deacon should be put to the *test* before he is given the *trust* to be a deacon.

Just what does it mean to be put to the test anyway? To be "tested" means that his walk is to be examined for evidence of faithfulness to the responsibilities he has been assigned. Jesus expressed this principle in Matthew 25:21: "…you were faithful over a few things, I will make you ruler over many things…" No man should be elected to the office of deacon if he has established a pattern of unfaithfulness in areas such as church attendance, tithing, sharing his faith, prayer and Bible study. Instead, he should be *proven* in all of these areas.

7. A deacon must be blameless. (1 Timothy 3:10) The term "blameless" implies that the person has not been *accused*. That is, there are no valid accusations being circulated that might indicate or point to problems with his character or conduct.

The word "blameless" also implies a conscience that is clear of conflict between himself and others. The Apostle Paul expressed it this way: "This being so, I myself always strive to have a conscience without offense toward God and men" (Acts 24:16). A blameless deacon has nothing in his life that Satan, the unsaved, or even a carnal Christian can use to criticize or attack him or the church. This does not mean that a blameless deacon is a perfect deacon; instead; it means that he is consistently seeking to live above reproach and to not bring embarrassment upon the cause of Christ.

8. A deacon must be a one-woman man. (1 Timothy 3:12) The "husband of one wife" is a man who is sexually pure and whose marriage commitment is to one woman only. We concede that some churches choose to interpret this verse to mean that the deacon is to be devoted to one woman at a time—that is, he is a "one-woman-kind-of-man." Others interpret it to mean that a deacon shall not have been divorced. Whatever the interpretation might be and however a church determines their position on it, the deacon is to morally clean and sexually pure.

As a pastor, I have chosen to stay with the stricter understanding and interpretation of this qualification—*that neither a deacon nor his spouse shall have been divorced*. In my years of ministry, I have concluded that there are plenty of opportunities to serve in the church, and pointing divorced men to these other service opportunities is both acceptable and commendable. One perfectly clear truth upon which all agree is this: A man who is not faithful to his wife should neither serve nor continue to serve as a deacon.

9. A deacon must be a good father. (1 Timothy 3:12) I believe that men who are known for "ruling their children…well" have an excellent background from which to serve as deacons. The implication here is not that their children must be perfect or without struggle, but that they have been nurtured correctly, instructed biblically, guided safely and disciplined appropriately. Scripture emphasizes the value of being a godly father: "The righteous man walks in his integrity; His children are blessed after him" (Proverbs 20:7).

10. A deacon must be the spiritual leader at home. (1 Timothy 3:12) Since the home is the basic, God-ordained unit of society, it is in the home that a deacon develops his spiritual leadership by setting a godly example, and by encouraging, understanding, loving and serving his wife and children. Note the leadership expectations that are common to the home and the church:

- Resolving conflict

- Building unity

- Maintaining love

- Serving each other

Here is a simple, yet profound maxim: *If you can be a good Christian at home, you can be a good Christian anywhere.* Struggles in the deacon's house will be reflected in struggles at the Lord's house. It is crucial, therefore, that churches ordain only those men whose homes reflect the peace and unity the church must have to flourish.

SUMMARY

As we have seen, being a deacon is an awesome responsibility. I believe this is the reason the Apostle Paul sets the qualifications for being a deacon in the larger context of being a pastor. In a real sense, deacons do the work of a pastor—by faithfully serving alongside him and supporting him as he leads the church.

Because a deacon serves with the pastor, he must meet the biblical qualifications required for honorable service. His personal character, family life and devotion to Christ come under the serious scrutiny of God's Word. This is only right because the church, after all, is the Body of Christ. Those who serve as deacons must be worthy of their calling.

DISCUSSION & APPLICATION

1. Before beginning this study, how did you view the importance of the deacon ministry in the local church? Have you ever been a part of vibrant deacon ministries in other churches? If so, what made them effective? Share together as a group.

   _____

   _____

2. The phrase "using the deacon ministry" means "to furnish that which is needed." What are some of the current needs your church is experiencing at this time, and how can your deacon body best assist in getting these needs met?

   _____

3. You may remember from the video lesson Pastor Johnny saying that during his years as a pastor, many deacons with whom he has served have become trusted friends, prayer partners and encouragers. How does this statement challenge or affirm the way you view the deacon ministry and your relationship to your pastor?

   _____

   _____

4. This lesson refers to deacon qualifications as a "very high standard," and that churches should "raise the bar" of leadership for deacons. Do you agree that the standard of character and conduct ought to be viewed as high as that of the pastor? In other words, should deacons be held to the same level of accountability as pastors? Why or why not?

   _____

   _____

5. Discuss as a group why Paul warns deacons not to be double-tongued. What does the term "double-tongued" suggest to you? Have you ever been involved with another deacon who often failed to keep his word? Without revealing names, discuss how it affected the other deacons and the church family?

   _____

   _____

6. Take a few moments now to compare the similarities of a deacon's leadership at home to his leadership at church. Why is it impossible for a deacon to be an effective leader at church when he is not an effective leader at home?

   _____

   _____

Carlton has served as a deacon in his local church for eight years, a church where many of his friends and family members attend. Needless to say, he was excited when he was first nominated and ordained as a deacon, but in recent years some of the excitement has faded, and being a deacon has become somewhat of a chore. Lately, Carlton has experienced some business setbacks that have motivated him to look for answers that have been hard to come by. As result of searching the Scriptures for direction and considering his position as a deacon, he is coming to grips with some glaring short-comings in his life, specifically in the areas of foul language, conduct at work, and his example at home. One day while having lunch with a business colleague who is also a deacon at the same church, Carlton shares his concerns and guilt feelings. The fellow deacon lightheartedly dismisses the matter by saying, "You know, Carlton, everyone has his faults. You're no worse than anyone else. We're all working on something, man. If you're asking for my advice, I'd tell you to chill out."

If you had been Carlton, how would you have responded to your fellow deacon? If you had been the fellow deacon Carlton confided in, how would you have responded to Carlton when he shared his concerns with you? Discuss as a group.

_____

_____

_____

_____

PRAYER OF COMMITMENT

Lord, I thank you for reminding me of how important it is for me to maintain godly character and conduct as a deacon in the church. I know there are areas where I need to make some changes, and I commit to you that I will do just that. I promise to take my role as a deacon seriously. I want to be all you want me to be. In Jesus' name, Amen.

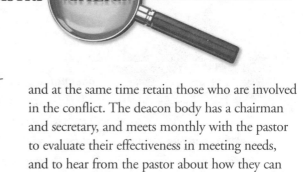

DEACON MINISTRY HIGHLIGHT

NOTE: Here is a church that is recognized for having an effective deacon ministry. If time permits, review the profile below as a group, then discuss any ideas or procedures you might apply in your own deacon ministry.

NORTHSIDE BAPTIST CHURCH
2501 N College Road
Wilmington, North Carolina 28405
(910) 791-6053
Kenny Chinn, Pastor

Church & Staff

Northside Baptist Church began as Murrayville Baptist Mission in July of 1956. In 1993, the church celebrated its 25th anniversary and voted to change its name to Northside Baptist Church. By 1994, the membership had grown to 695, and the next year Reverend Kenneth W. Chinn was called as pastor. During the years that followed, Pastor Chinn led the church to three morning services and three Sunday Schools, an AWANA program, and a music ministry for all ages, including a 96-member adult choir. NSBC continues a tradition of acquiring neighboring properties to expand its facilities to meet current and future needs. Today, NBCW has a member of over 2,000, worship attendance of around 1,000, and an average Sunday School attendance of around 800. In addition to Pastor Chinn, the staff includes an associate pastor, along with ministers of education, music, youth, pastoral care, and pastoral projects.

Deacon Organization & Ministry

The 19 deacons at Northside serve primarily to maintain unity and harmony in the church. One of the church's commitments to unity is that no conflicts can arise that will not be addressed quickly, preferably before the next scheduled assembly of the church for worship. While deacons serve in a variety of ministries, they try to address conflicts or signs of disharmony while they are small, resolve them before they become big, and at the same time retain those who are involved in the conflict. The deacon body has a chairman and secretary, and meets monthly with the pastor to evaluate their effectiveness in meeting needs, and to hear from the pastor about how they can best facilitate the future goals of the ministry. Pastor Chinn also takes this opportunity to coach the deacons on skills necessary for ministering to a diverse church family and community.

Deacon Qualifications & Selection Process

Deacon candidates are nominated by the church body and then interviewed by current deacons— with the pastor's approval— to evaluate their qualifications for service. After demonstrating the necessary qualifications and commitment to the ministry through a written questionnaire, deacon candidates continue the interview process until ordination is approved. Ordained deacons at NBCW serve for an indefinite period of time determined by service, conduct and commitment. The deacon body is self-governing by approval of the pastor, which means that they hold themselves to a high standard of conduct and service, and determine if one of their number needs to step down from his deacon role for any reason.

Success Factors

Pastor Chinn enjoys a wonderful ministry relationship with the Northside deacons and considers them to be his personal friends. The joy of being a deacon at Northside comes from serving in the biblical model for a church that is growing and alive with the activity of God. The deacons know that meeting needs and maintaining unity is critical to the church's ability to reach people with the Gospel. Helping keep the church on mission and then seeing the results in the baptismal pool make serving as a deacon at Northside a fulfilling experience.

2

THE DEACON AND HIS WORK

His Mission, His Responsibilities and His Mentoring

INTRODUCTION

Personally, I cannot think of a more exciting position to be called to in today's church than that of a deacon. But deacon service is not just a *position* to hold; it is a *mission* to fulfill and a *work* to be done. Acts 6:1-4 is the key passage for this lesson. This text captures the core work of a deacon in the local church.

> *Now in those days, when the number of the disciples was multiplying, there arose a complaint against the Hebrews by the Hellenists, because their widows were neglected in the daily distribution. Then the twelve summoned the multitude of the disciples and said, 'It is not desirable that we should leave the word of God and serve tables.'*

> *'Therefore, brethren, seek out from among you seven men of good reputation, full of the Holy Spirit and wisdom, whom we may appoint over this business; but we will give ourselves continually to prayer and to the ministry of the word.'* (Acts 6:1-4)

Though seven men were chosen, they are not actually called "deacons" in this passage. Their selection, however, shows the initial action of the church to choose men who would help the apostles by serving the church body. Scholars believe that this text represents the earliest recorded activity of deacons. The five reasons the early church needed deacons indicates the kind of work they were assigned to accomplish.

REASONS TO SERVE—WORK TO BE ACCOMPLSHED

To Handle Church Growth

A church experiences growing pains much like a child as he or she is growing up and experiencing changing needs. When the church grows, the needs grow, costs grow, and someone must pay the price for that growth. Growth may require a church to go to multiple services or Sunday Schools, enter a building program, buy more land, create more parking, add staff, and expand ministries. Growth demands change, and growth changes things. The key is to grow steadily rather than to decline steadily.

The early church faced difficulties as a result of growing pains. Glancing back to the beginning of Acts, we see the explanation for the wonderful growth recorded in chapter six where Jesus' prophecy was being fulfilled.

> *But you shall receive power when the Holy Spirit has come upon you; and you shall be witnesses to Me in Jerusalem, and in all Judea and Samaria, and to the end of the earth.* (Acts 1:8)

By the time of Acts chapter six, the early church had saturated Jerusalem with the Gospel. They had also influenced the neighboring communities and were positioned to evangelize Samaria. When the apostles became bogged down serving the growing congregation with virtually no help, they added the office of the deacon. The early church didn't change in order to grow; it changed because it was growing.

Following Jesus' clear instructions, the goal of the early church was to take the Gospel to the whole world. It is no less our goal as well today. The apostles made a wise decision in appointing these seven men for service, and because they were appointed, the church was better able to grow in faith and be faithful in service.

To Protect Church Harmony

"Hebrews" refers to Jewish disciples of Christ who spoke the Hebrew language, while "Hellenists" were Jewish converts from Greek-speaking lands (verse 1). These "Hellenists" had come to Jerusalem for Pentecost but had stayed with their new family of faith rather than return home.

> Growth demands change, and growth changes things. The key is to grow steadily rather than to decline steadily.

Because of the "complaint" that arose between these two groups, the early church was vulnerable to a church split. Church splits often occur because people are dissatisfied or complaining. Deacons have a great responsibility to help maintain church harmony. Jesus prayed for the unity of His disciples: "I do not pray for these alone, but also for those who will believe in me through their word; that they all may be one, as you, Father, are in me, and I in you; that they also may be one in us, that the world may believe that you sent me" (John 17:20-21).

Complaining can destroy the unity of the church.

The Greek word "*koinonia*" was a special word used to describe the communion (fellowship or harmonious relationship) enjoyed by the early church. Just as Christians have communion because of their common bond in Jesus Christ, deacons should be "endeavoring to keep the unity of the Spirit in the bond of peace" (Ephesians 4:3).

To Provide for the Needy

The need for deacons arose because of the needs of people, and the apostles demonstrated just how important people are by ensuring that those needs were met. A single yet profound truth to remember is: "God loves people more than anything." And deacons surely ought to love what God loves. Churches have an obligation to assist in meeting the legitimate needs of their members.

> *Pure and undefiled religion before God and the Father is this: to visit orphans and widows in their trouble, and to keep oneself unspotted from the world.* (James 1:27)

Since deacons are called to meet the needs of people, they ought to do so faithfully so the pastor can do what he has been called to do. Pastors are truly blessed when they are surrounded by deacons who are serious about service. The pastor has a built-in desire to minister to every member of the church, but because this is usually not possible to do, deacons are called on to assist. The pastor, therefore, can lead in confidence knowing that the people's needs are being met just as if he were doing it himself.

To Prioritize the Ministry

The principle that guided the apostles' decision to appoint seven men to serve was a simple understanding that the church needed to work *together* to be effective in ministry. Their motto might read: *None of us can do alone what all of us can do together.*

With deacons in place to serve tables, the apostles were set free to prioritize the ministry. For them, nothing could override their responsibility in giving themselves "continually to prayer and to the ministry of the Word." As a pastor, one of the highlights of my ministry is the prayer time I have with our deacons on Sunday morning before our services begin. In those brief moments I can pour out my heart and personal needs knowing that these men will pray for me and assist me in the work of ministry.

In addition, when the deacons serve the needs of the congregation, the pastor is given the time to spend in the Word, preparing to deliver a "thus saith the Lord" every time he stands to preach. Plus, he is able to spend time discipling and mentoring those individuals who feel that God may be calling them into some type of vocational ministry.

People may know the latest headlines, and they may have heard one talking head after another speak his mind about this or that issue. But when these same people show up at church, they want to know from their pastor if God has anything special to say to them that will help them live a meaningful and abundant life today. Only the pastor who has been alone with God can deliver on this requirement. Hopefully, every pastor is fortunate enough to have deacons serving alongside him who minister to the needs of the people so he can have time with the Word of God and prayer.

To Ensure Gospel Penetration

Because the apostles kept their priorities, and the appointed men served the people, the church experienced great results.

- The word of God increased.

- The number of disciples multiplied.

- A great company of priests was obedient to the faith.

The important lesson to learn is that when ministry is conducted appropriately, the church grows exponentially. Deacons who base their ministry on the blueprint given in Acts 6:1-4 will be growing in their faith and faithful in their service.

SUMMARY

No church exists that does not face difficulties, and usually one man alone cannot handle them. This is the context we observe in Acts 6:1-4 that leads to the appointment of deacons in the church. Deacons were to be men of the highest character and deepest commitment who were poised to keep peace in the congregation while serving the people. As a result, the apostles set themselves to continually pray and seek God. Their preaching became more powerful than ever because they did not have to leave the Word of God and serve tables. As a result, the church experienced growth. Faithful deacons serving the Lord by serving the people were largely responsible for the new growth.

> Deacons have a great responsibility to help maintain church harmony.

DISCUSSION & APPLICATION

1. The 1st century church grew in spite of internal problems. Think about similar problems you have seen in churches you have attended or served. How were the problems handled, and what was the result? How did the deacon ministry help or how could it have helped? How might things have turned out differently?

    _____

    _____

2. Is the church you serve changing because it is growing or does it need to change in order to grow? What are the barriers to change in your church, if any? How can the deacons help facilitate this change so that growth can occur? As you discover potential opportunities through this exercise, make a list of them. You will want to meet with your pastor and discuss these ideas.

    _____

    _____

3. Consider for a moment the harmony or unity of the church you serve. Since unity is the catalyst for church growth, discuss in a positive way any issues that may be hindering or threatening church unity. Make a list of these issues, and seek the pastor's counsel on how the deacons can work together to overcome them.

    _____

    _____

4. Since Scripture is clear that the deacons are to serve the church, discuss the current responsibilities of deacons in your church. Make a list of them on a white board or in the space below. Put a check mark by those responsibilities that you feel good about and a question mark by those that may need attention. Discuss a plan of action.

    _____

    _____

    _____

    _____

5. Consider the physical needs of the church family and prospects in your community. Are these needs being met? What ministries, functions, or special events might the deacon body develop to help meet community needs and reach prospects? Think outside the box and make notes.

    _____

    _____

6. Think for a moment about the relationship between the pastor and the deacons in your church. Is the relationship healthy and developing steadily in a positive way? Or is the relationship somewhat strained, perhaps needing to be renewed? What can you do in a non-threatening way as a group to refocus on the "main things" and get your focus off personalities and past conflicts that may be hindering the spirit of the body? After all, what is the real work to be done based on Scripture, and who is to do it in unity and harmony?

_____

_____

LifeScene

Pastor John Krate serves a church of 400 members in the Midwest. He has been there about two and a half years, really loves the people, and sees a lot of potential for future growth. Pastor Krate really wants the church to grasp his vision and passion for the lost, and he has many ideas for ways to reach prospects in their community through service opportunities, special events and Sunday School. Unfortunately, few people in the church share his passion, especially those with influence. Ray Smith, chairman of deacons and a member of the finance committee, cannot understand why Pastor Krate is so concerned with growing the church. Additional people will create growing pains, add expenses, overcrowd classrooms and the auditorium—not to mention create more parking problems. One day Ray tells Pastor Krate, "You just preach the Word, visit the hospitals, and see to the marrying and burying, and let us take care of the rest. We'll be fine." Pastor Krate is frustrated, but knows in his heart that the Lord has called him to lead this church. He is committed to seeing it through no matter what, but desperately needs someone to talk to.

If Pastor Krate came to you for advice, what would you tell him? What would you say to Ray? How could you try to influence change in the church without creating disunity? Discuss this situation as a group and note any similarities that may exist in your own church.

_____

_____

_____

_____

PRAYER OF COMMITMENT

Father, I come to you with a humble heart and a sincere desire to be a deacon who accomplishes the work assigned to me. Help me to submit myself to you, my pastor and this dear church family you have called me to serve. As I serve, I am going to try my best to put you first, others second and myself last. In Jesus' name, Amen.

DEACON MINISTRY HIGHLIGHT

NOTE: Here is a church that is recognized for having an effective deacon ministry. If time permits, review the profile below as a group, then discuss any ideas or procedures you might apply in your own deacon ministry.

FIRST BAPTIST CHURCH
SAN JACINTO

841 East Evans St.

San Jacinto, California 92583

(951) 654-4411

**Stacy Johnson and Bret Capranica,
Co-pastors**

Church & Staff

First Baptist Church San Jacinto has been a predominantly Caucasian senior adult fellowship located in a working class community with very few middle-aged and single adults, and very few teenagers. Recently, however, it has been attracting diverse young couples with children. When Stacy Johnson became pastor in 1999, the church embarked on an exciting period of growth. In 2002, Bret Capranica joined the church staff as associate pastor, and in 2003 became co-pastor, sharing equal authority and responsibility with Pastor Johnson. The two co-pastors, a full-time student pastor, and two lay pastors (formerly full-time pastors) make up the pastors' council that meets weekly to provide direction and ministry oversight for the congregation. Each member of the council has specific duties within the church. FBCSJ currently has a membership of 162, an average worship attendance of 225, and an average of 162 in Sunday School.

Deacon Organization & Ministry

FBCSJ is currently reorganizing their deacon ministry and selecting new deacons to carry out the work of existing ministries, help the pastors with oversight and administration of the membership, and make sure ministries function effectively. The ministries assigned to the deacons will include corporate worship services, audio needs, church facilities, Sunday School, Ministry Institute of Training, children and student ministries, finances, missions, and women's ministries.

Deacon Qualifications & Selection Process

Deacons are nominated by the FBCSJ church members and are then reviewed by the pastors to comprise a list of men who meet biblical qualifications. These names are then submitted to the church membership for affirmation and ordination. Ordained deacons are assigned to one of the members of the pastors' council to serve with that specific pastor in the ministries he oversees.

Success Factors

The deacons and their families at FBCSJ enjoy a close personal relationship with their assigned pastor, one of whose assignments is to disciple the deacons. Serving as ministry assistants to the pastors enables the deacons to use their gifts and abilities to accomplish the objectives set forth by the pastors. As servant leaders rather than administrators, the deacons of FBCSJ enable their pastors to focus on prayer, Bible study, sermon and service preparation, outreach, and leadership of the congregation. The church recognizes the value of implementing this kind of deacon ministry, knowing that selecting men of the highest qualifications is critical to their future growth.

CHAPTER

3

THE DEACON AND HIS WIFE

Her Attributes, Her Ministry and Their Home Together

INTRODUCTION

I know you'd agree with me that the contribution your wife makes to you and your home is priceless. And this is especially true when you are a pastor or a deacon. To say that a deacon's wife plays a vital role in her husband's ministry is an understatement. I've heard it said that no one prevents a deacon from walking with Christ, but if anyone could, it would be his wife. Yet at the same time, no one can be a greater encouragement to a deacon than his wife.

Like it or not, when a man becomes a deacon, his wife is elevated to a position in the church where more is expected of her. I like to think of her influence as a fragrance of encouragement that extends from her innermost being into the life and ministry of her husband and to all with whom she comes into contact. She can bring great joy to his service and at the same time bring joy to everyone around her. Let it be said that the value of a godly, supportive wife is incalculable.

TWO CHALLENGING PRINCIPLES

Many sermons have been preached on the qualifications of a deacon, but very few on the qualifications of the deacon's wife. Yet the Bible is not silent about the deacon's wife. Instead, it speaks clearly of her attributes, her ministry, and the home she shares together with her husband. As we explore the qualities of a deacon's wife in this lesson, keep the following statements in mind:

• A deacon's wife needs to share the *same calling* with her husband.

• A deacon's wife needs to have the *same character* as her husband.

GENERAL QUALITIES FOR ALL CHRISTIAN WIVES

"He who finds a wife finds a good thing, and obtains favor from the Lord" (Proverbs 18:22). Even more is written about a good wife in Proverbs 31:10-31 where she is described as having most every virtue that wisdom offers. Let's note the entire passage.

10) Who can find a virtuous wife? For her worth is far above rubies.

11) The heart of her husband safely trusts her; so he will have no lack of gain.

12) She does him good and not evil all the days of her life.

13) She seeks wool and flax, and willingly works with her hands.

14) She is like the merchant ships, she brings her food from afar.

15) *She also rises while it is yet night, and provides food for her household, and a portion for her maidservants.*

16) *She considers a field and buys it; from her profits she plants a vineyard.*

17) *She girds herself with strength, and strengthens her arms.*

18) *She perceives that her merchandise is good, and her lamp does not go out by night.*

19) *She stretches out her hands to the distaff, and her hand holds the spindle.*

20) *She extends her hand to the poor, yes, she reaches out her hands to the needy.*

21) *She is not afraid of snow for her household, for all her household is clothed with scarlet.*

22) *She makes tapestry for herself; her clothing is fine linen and purple.*

23) *Her husband is known in the gates, when he sits among the elders of the land.*

24) *She makes linen garments and sells them, and supplies sashes for the merchants.*

25) *Strength and honor are her clothing; she shall rejoice in time to come.*

26) *She opens her mouth with wisdom, and on her tongue is the law of kindness.*

27) *She watches over the ways of her household, and does not eat the bread of idleness.*

28) *Her children rise up and call her blessed; her husband also, and he praises her:*

29) *"Many daughters have done well, but you excel them all."*

30) *Charm is deceitful and beauty is passing, but a woman who fears the Lord, she shall be praised.*

31) *Give her of the fruit of her hands, and let her own works praise her in the gates.*

From this lengthy but beautiful passage about the godly woman, we discover four general qualities of a good wife.

1. The Treasures of a Good Wife (verses 10-12).
A good wife is a *virtuous* woman. The writer uses the word "virtuous" which means integrity and moral strength. A good wife is strong in all moral qualities. She is also a *valuable* woman to her husband and family. The word "worth" speaks of her preciousness.

Ruth is the only woman in the Old Testament who is called a "virtuous woman" (Ruth 3:11). The prayer of every deacon's wife ought to be "Lord, make me a virtuous woman." Solomon would have given a king's ransom for a woman like Ruth.

To what does the Bible connect the value of a good wife? It connects her value with her *love*. Verse 11 contains a phrase that describes the heart of a deacon for his wife – "the heart of her husband safely trusts her." A deacon has great confidence in serving when he can safely trust his wife. Trust is one of the most important elements in a relationship. Allow that trust to be destroyed, and you will struggle the rest of your life in your marital relationship.

2. The Thrust of a Good Wife (verses 13-22).
Note that a good wife does a *compassionate work* (verse 13). The fact that she "willingly works" implies that she is not serving her husband or her church out of forced obligation; instead she is serving out of calling and passion. As a result, she has busy hands. A deacon's wife allows God to take the capacity she has and use it outside the home to bless the church family her husband serves as deacon.

A good wife also does a *commendable work* (verses 14-22). Verses 14 through 22 describe the activities of the good wife, and those activities display the following qualities of her character:

- She is not lazy.

- She is health-conscious and energetic.

- She is generous.

3. The Truths of a Good Wife (verses 23-26). A good and godly wife is a *compliment* to her husband (verse 23). "Her husband is known in the gates" because his wife encourages his strengths, helps his weaknesses, counsels him wisely, builds up his confidence, helps mold his character, and gently smoothes his path.

Furthermore, a good and godly wife imparts *confidence* to her husband (verses 25-26). These verses move from what a good woman does with her *hands* to what is in her *heart*. Among her greatest assets is "wisdom," the ability to live life skillfully. Additionally, "the law of kindness on her lips" is held back from no one. A deacon's wife who is full of wisdom and kindness will bring great benefit to her husband's life and ministry.

4. The Testimony of a Good Wife (verses 27-31). As far as her family is concerned, she is the greatest wife and mother in the world. A good wife, therefore, deserves adoration (verses 29-30). In fact, appreciation is inadequate, so the writer proclaims "you have excelled them all," meaning that there is none better. The best wife a man can have is one who fears the Lord.

SPECIFIC QUALITIES OF THE DEACON'S WIFE

Likewise, their wives must be reverent, not slanderers, temperate, faithful in all things. (1 Timothy 3:11)

A deacon's wife should be reverent. Placing the qualities of a deacon's wife in the same text as the qualifications for a pastor and a deacon shows just how important her role is. The word "reverent" means that the deacon's wife should be serious about her calling; she can *help* her husband to serve as deacon or *hinder* her husband from serving as deacon. "Reverent" also means that the deacon's wife demonstrates self-respect in her conduct. The Apostle Paul stated that he was careful to keep his conscience clear with God and with others so there would be no barriers to making God known.

A deacon's wife should be responsible. The word "devil" is translated from the same word as the word "slanderer" in 1 Timothy 3:8. "Slanderer" also means "double-tongued" and refers to one who is given to finding fault with others. This type of divisive conduct is simply irresponsible and may severely damage the unity of a church.

Remember, the deacon ministry began in response to a need that was causing division. A deacon's wife would be hypocritical to engage in conduct that creates the same problem she is responsible for preventing. Here are three principles to help guard against being double-tongued.

- How one discusses another person's character discloses one's own character.

- An irresponsible wife easily disqualifies a potential deacon.

- A deacon's wife manages her opinions and her concerns responsibly.

A deacon's wife should be reasonable. The word "temperate" conveys the idea that the deacon's wife must be sober in judgment and have self-control by not cheapening the ministry or the gospel message by foolish behavior. "Temperate" also means to have a serious attitude and earnestness toward the deacon's work. "Temperate" can also mean vigilant, an attitude which can be expressed in the four ways: 1) being practical; 2) being sensible; 3) being logical; and 4) being fair in dealing with others.

> Let it be said that the value of a godly, supportive wife is incalculable.

A deacon's wife should be reliable. The word "reliable" means "faithful in all things," and can be used both in both a passive sense and an active sense. The passive sense means that others can rely on her. The active sense means that she relies on God and those He has placed in authority over her in leading the church.

SUMMARY

The expression "the deacon's wife I want to be" implies that the wife of a deacon wants to grow in faith and be faithful in service just like her husband. There is simply no way to place a value on a wife who is a good and godly woman. She is priceless. And together with her husband, they will prove to be strong servants of the Lord for years to come.

DISCUSSION & APPLICATION

1. The introduction of this lesson states that church members expect a higher standard of conduct from a deacon's wife because of the husband's position. Do you think this expectation exists in the church you serve, and if so, do you think it is reasonable? Why or why not?

   _____

   _____

2. When considering prospective deacons, how is the character of the wife typically evaluated in your church? Is she part of the interview process, or is some other method used to determine if she has the desirable qualities for a deacon's wife?

   _____

   _____

3. Would you ordain someone to be a deacon if you got the feeling that his wife felt that his or her ministry expectations would be too great? What if the deacon candidate desired the position very much and assured you that his wife's attitude would not be a problem?

   _____

   _____

4. Situations like medical emergencies, bereavements, and special events can really disrupt a deacon's time at home with his family. How can a deacon's wife support her husband when the demands of the ministry are unexpected or time consuming? How can the deacon body minister to a wife who is less than supportive?

   _____

   _____

5. Ask each deacon (and his wife, if present) to list the four qualities of a deacon's wife in the order of importance to them. This exercise could also be done in small groups. Once everyone has finished prioritizing their answers, discuss the results.

   _____

   _____

6. When and how do the wives of deacons in your church get together for fellowship and discipleship? Would it be a good idea for them to have an annual retreat or meet occasionally during the year? How would this be beneficial to the deacons and their wives?

   _____

   _____

7. What should the relationship between a deacon and his wife look like anyway? What words does the Bible use to describe their relationship? What are signs of an unhealthy relationship in a deacon's home? How can the deacon group as a whole help a fellow deacon and his wife if serious problems develop in their relationship?

_____

_____

It is deacon nomination time again at The Church in the Mountains, and two fine men have are being considered for nomination. Don has been married for 12 years, has a stellar reputation as a godly man whose wife is exemplary in every way. Carol is active in the church, teaching third grade girls, singing in the choir and serving wherever needed. James has been married 14 years and also has a stellar reputation as a godly man with much ability and willingness to serve. James' wife Patty volunteers in the preschool department and is available to help whenever she hears of a need in the church. She is known, however, for being outspoken, loud, and opinionated if the church as a body makes a decision she doesn't agree with. Sometimes she prefers discussing matters publicly instead of privately. When Patty is upset about something at church or at home, people are going to hear about it.

If you were on the deacon nominating committee interviewing James and Don, how would the behavior of their wives determine your decision about ordaining them? Would James' wife's behavior prevent him from becoming a deacon? If so, what could or should happen in the future to make it possible for James to be ordained as a deacon?

_____

_____

_____

_____

PRAYER OF COMMITMENT

Dear Lord, thank you for my wife and for revealing once again to both of us just how important her role is. Help us to understand that our character and conduct as a deacon and wife are to be exemplary and that you can use us to reach many people for Christ. Help me to serve her and our family well as I seek to serve you. In Jesus' name, Amen.

DEACON MINISTRY HIGHLIGHT

NOTE: Here is a church that is recognized for having an effective deacon ministry. If time permits, review the profile below as a group, then discuss any ideas or procedures you might apply in your own deacon ministry.

PRESTONWOOD BAPTIST CHURCH

6801 W. Park Blvd.

Plano, Texas 75093

(972) 820-5000

Jack Graham, Pastor

Church & Staff

Prestonwood Baptist Church began meeting in a city recreation center on February 6, 1977, and continued to meet there until its first building was completed on February 24, 1979. To accommodate the rapid growth that followed, the church expanded into nearby theaters, office buildings, a country club, storefronts and temporary buildings. After additional facilities were added, Prestonwood was soon running over 4,500 in Sunday School. Dr. Jack Graham became senior pastor in 1989, and in 1994, began to lead the church to relocate to a 138-acre site in Plano. Today the church has a membership of over 26,000, with 13,000 in worship and over 9,000 in Sunday School. Prestonwood Church and Prestonwood Christian Academy have a combined staff of 770, with 32 full-time ministers serving the main church campus and the north church campus.

Deacon Organization & Ministry

One hundred and fifty-seven active deacons and 120 inactive deacons serve the church family at PBC. Officers include chairman, vice chairman, secretary, treasurer, and communications officer. Deacons at PBC serve on "ministry teams" to accomplish responsibilities in the areas of prison ministry, hospital visits, local missions, homebound, and special projects, as well as the observance of The Lord's Supper. Pastor Graham provides leadership to the deacon officers and vision to the deacon body through monthly meetings, which are open to all active and inactive deacons.

Deacon Qualifications & Selection Process

PBC deacons are nominated and selected by a vote of the church body and then serve a 3-year term after which they can be placed in an inactive status. Future 3-year terms for inactive deacons are subject to the same process of nomination and church vote.

Success Factors

Carrying out the biblical deacon ministry model is the major goal of the deacons at Prestonwood, enabling them to serve a large, growing fellowship and take the Gospel to the community and the world. Every deacon is accountable to deacon officers and team leaders for the completion of his assigned tasks, promoting unity within the church, all the while maintaining balance in his home and professional life. The deacons at Prestonwood agree that there is no greater joy than serving the Lord in harmony alongside the pastor.

THE DEACON AND HIS WORSHIP

His Faithfulness to the Word, the Church, to Prayer and Praise

INTRODUCTION

As much as I love to preach and teach the Word of God each week in our church and around the country, I can assure you that without a regular schedule of public and private worship of the Lord Jesus Christ I would be totally ineffective as a pastor and preacher of the Gospel. I simply have to worship. I cannot live and function without it.

"Worship" is a compound word that means to "give worth." Worshipping God acknowledges that He is worthy of what we are giving. God *demands* our worship, *deserves* our worship and *desires* our worship. What is the result of sincere worship? A yielded and obedient heart.

The Bible has a lot to say about worship, and Jesus was specific in what he had to say about it.

> *But the hour is coming, and now is, when the true worshippers will worship the Father in spirit and truth…and those who worship him must worship in spirit and truth.* (John 4:23-24)

> *Behold, I stand at the door and knock. If anyone hears my voice and opens the door, I will come in to him and dine with him, and he with me.* (Revelation 3:20)

God is standing and knocking at the door of our heart, desiring not only to speak to us but also to spend time with us. As spiritual leaders, deacons have a need to worship God in spirit and in truth, and *two aspects of worship* must exist for a deacon to be faithful to the Word, to the church, and to prayer and praise:

A Deacon and His Private Worship

As spiritual leaders, our private time alone with God should be the top priority of every day. If a deacon is not having regular communion with the God he serves, how can he ever hope to fulfill his calling? Deacons cannot lead others where they are not going themselves.

A deacon, therefore, must be a worshipper if he hopes to help others become worshippers. Personal time alone with God was Jesus' habit. Habits are often thought of negatively, but habits can be positive. A deacon can have no better habit than beginning each day with the Lord. Note the habit of Jesus.

> *And in the morning, rising up a great while before day, he went out, and departed into a solitary place, and there prayed.* (Mark 1:35)

The times of our *corporate* worship are only as good as the accumulation of the individual times of our *private* worship. It is one thing to come to worship on Sunday, and it is quite another to bring our worship with us. Several things ought to be involved in *private* worship:

- To be in conversation with God—honest confession, gratitude, and intercession for others

- To be in communion with God—the Word of God aligning my thoughts with His through encouragement and correction

- To be consumed by God—God responding to my private worship in a personal way that lifts my heart

Private worship leads to personal purity. Purity, in turn, empowers public service. To be the deacon you want to be, you must realize that nothing ranks higher than personal purity. If you miss in the area of personal purity, everything else falls by the wayside.

> One of the greatest blessings a deacon can bestow on his pastor is to pray with him and for him.

The Deacon and His Public Worship

It just makes sense that a deacon should attend and participate in the events his church deems important. And what is more important than the worship services where the congregation gathers for music and praise, prayer, Bible preaching, offering, fellowship as a church body, and a time of personal decision and commitment? A deacon should be faithful in worship.

Deacons and pastors are the only church officers mentioned in the New Testament, and they share equal responsibility in promoting and attending church services. Since no group ever rises above its leadership, pastors and deacons should set the example for faithful attendance. In so doing, they will be raising the standard for the rest of the church family to follow their example.

An important part of public worship is the giving of tithes and offerings and a deacon should be faithful to this part of public worship. A man should not be considered for ordination as a deacon if he does not contribute financial support to his own church.

Jesus said, "For where your treasure is, there will your heart be also" (Matthew 6:21). So the faithfulness of a man in giving to the church he serves is one of the clearest indicators of his true attitude toward the church. How can a deacon serve a church when his heart is not in it? It will be very difficult for a pastor to lead church members to give faithfully when their deacons are not setting the example.

Prayer is another significant part of public worship and a deacon must be faithful in prayer. Like private worship, a deacon must practice private prayer during the week if he is to be effective in his public prayers on Sunday. Because they share spiritual leadership in the church, deacons and pastors ought to be the most faithful prayer warriors in the church, praying for the needs of the people. One of the greatest blessings a deacon can bestow on his pastor is to pray with him and for him.

Deacons should also be sensitive to those who attend public worship services. God may use a deacon more while he is on his way to a service than when he is in his normal place of service. A deacon's opportunities to serve can occur in the most unexpected places. Jesus said that the two greatest commandments were to love God and to love others (Matthew 22:34-40). We show our love to God during public worship services, but those services do not necessarily provide the opportunity to show our love to others as much as other times of personal ministry. The Good Samaritan (Luke 10:30-37) showed his love and concern not in a worship setting but in a roadside setting.

Gaining the office of deacon and *fulfilling* the office through faithful, practical service are two entirely different things. Possible areas of service include:

- Hospitality – ushers and greeters

- Outreach and evangelism

- Benevolence ministry

- Music Ministry

- Administering The Lord's Supper

- Assisting with baptism

- Altar counseling

- Bible teaching

Finally, a deacon should be faithful in his support of the pastor. This partnership is on full display during invitation time of the Sunday service. As the pastor extends the invitation for commitment after his message, the deacons should be available to graciously assist those who respond. There's no more meaningful experience than taking someone by the hand and leading them into a personal relationship with the Jesus Christ. The church will have its highest expression of worship when pastor and deacons serve God in a loving partnership.

SUMMARY

Everything God wants a deacon to be—as well as everything a deacon wants to be—extends from his heart as a sincere worshipper of God. A deacon's *private* worship life energizes his *public* worship life with a vibrant faith that overflows to the people he serves. Worship is the key to being an effective deacon.

DISCUSSION & APPLICATION

1. What words/thoughts came to mind when you heard that God demands our worship, deserves our worship, and desires our worship? Share together for a few moments what worship means to you and how you express worship.

   _____

   _____

2. An excellent time for private worship and mediation is the early morning hours. Share with one another about your private time with the Lord, when you observe it and what it means to you. What are some of the results you experience?

   _____

   _____

3. A.W. Tozer said, "We're here to be worshippers first and workers second. We take a convert and immediately make a worker out of him. God never meant it to be so. God meant that a convert should learn to be a worshipper, and after that he can learn to be a worker…the work done by a worshipper will have eternity in it." How does this statement apply to a deacon and his service?

   _____

   _____

4. True or false: "We tend to become like the object of our worship." What examples or thoughts come to mind when we contemplate this statement?

   _____

   _____

5. Is worship more than a Sunday event to attend? If so, how and why?

_____

_____

6. What is it about Sunday morning worship that makes it such a significant part of a Christian's spiritual life? Are there other worship opportunities at your church that are meaningful to you? If so, mention them.

_____

_____

7. Jesus said, "But the hour is coming, and now is, when the true worshippers will worship the Father in spirit and truth…and those who worship Him must worship in spirit and truth" (John 4:23-24). What do you think Jesus meant by this? What implications does this have on our church's corporate worship?

_____

_____

8. The video lesson refers to a deacon's faithfulness in giving. How does a deacon's giving reflect his attitude toward the church he serves? Think about your own giving: Do you feel good about what you are giving to the Lord? Share together some of the blessings you have received by giving your tithes and offerings.

_____

_____

As spiritual leaders, our private
time alone with God should be the
top priority of every day.

Harold and Betty have been long-time, faithful members of the church, but lately they have grown concerned with the direction the worship it taking: the music seems too loud; the songs are unfamiliar; and a growing number of young adults have been closing their eyes and lifting their hands during worship—even shouting occasionally. Plus, Harold and Betty get tired of standing so long during the music. "Why can't we sit down every now and then?" they whisper to each other. While Harold is slowly adapting to the new worship style, Betty continues to think that church services should be quiet, reverent, and sacred. She reads biblical accounts (Daniel 1:12-17 and Revelation 1:12-17) where godly men responded with great fear and awe. People raising their hands and speaking out loud during the services really bothers her. She thinks it's downright distracting and just makes her feel uncomfortable. She doesn't know if it will do any good, but she decides to talk to someone who has some influence and tell them that she's not the only one who feels this way.

If Betty knew you were a deacon and sought you out to share her concerns with you, what would you tell her and how would you try to help her? Discuss together how you might handle the situation.

_____

_____

_____

_____

PRAYER OF COMMITMENT

Dear Lord, I realize that you want true worshippers, and I want to be one. I am understanding more and more how important my service as a deacon is, and I know that I cannot serve well if I am not worshipping you with all my heart. I pray that the worship I experience in public will extend from the overflow of the worship I experience in private so that my life and service might bring glory and honor to you. In Jesus' name, Amen.

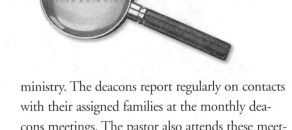

DEACON MINISTRY HIGHLIGHT

NOTE: Here is a church that is recognized for having an effective deacon ministry. If time permits, review the profile below as a group, then discuss any ideas or procedures you might apply in your own deacon ministry.

FIRST BAPTIST CHURCH CHIPLEY

1300 South Boulevard
Chipley, Florida 32428
(850) 638-1830
Mike Orr, Pastor

Church & Staff

First Baptist Chipley was started in 1887 with 19 charter members who built their first permanent facility in 1902. The church relocated to its current site in the center of the beautiful Florida panhandle in 1979 and began playing a major role in the life of the surrounding community through lay ministries and involvement with students. FBCC is a mostly Caucasian congregation but has African-American and Hispanic members and visitors representative of the surrounding area. Mike Orr became pastor of First Baptist Chipley in June of 2000, and the church has grown steadily under his leadership. Church membership is now around 1,000. FBCC averages 600 in its two Sunday morning services and 440 in Sunday School. Pastor Orr's full-time staff members include music and administration minister, education minister, student minister, and a music associate.

Deacon Organization & Ministry

First Baptist Chipley currently has 22 deacons in service, in a structure that includes a chairman, vice-chairman, secretary, and committee chairmen. The various committees —or teams—are service-oriented, not administrative-oriented. Deacons at FBCC are assigned church families and members with whom they are to stay in contact and provide ministry. The deacons report regularly on contacts with their assigned families at the monthly deacons meetings. The pastor also attends these meetings to discuss ministry, vision, and to spend time in prayer.

Deacon Qualifications & Selection Process

At FBCC, church members nominate candidates for the deacon ministry, and the staff and deacon body review the nominations to select which ones to interview. The interview process includes discussion of biblical qualifications, expectations and commitment required to be a deacon. Deacon candidates who (along with their wives) meet the standards and are willing to commit to these expectations are then submitted to the church body for a vote at the next scheduled church business meeting. Ordained deacons at FBCC serve a 3-year term.

Success Factors

The deacons at First Baptist Chipley are not administrators, but ministry assistants who support the pastor and staff whole-heartedly by ministering to the church body and reaching out to the unchurched through partnerships with the Sunday School classes. Deacon body objectives are to meet the ministry needs of the church and community, encourage outreach, contact all church members at least once a quarter, and participate in the various ministries of the church. Pastor Orr and his staff enjoy a positive relationship with the deacons as they work together for kingdom growth. FBCC deacons are willing to adapt and change as necessary to achieve their goals.

THE DEACON AND HIS WALK

His Application of Kingdom Principles for Daily Living

INTRODUCTION

In a day when the media is bombarding us on every front through gadgets we can hold in our hands, carry in our pockets, or attach to our ears, it is easy to lose sight of the life-changing effects of *kingdom work and living*. As a word of caution: regardless of what is going on in our world today—politics, the war on terror, rising costs on every front—we must never underestimate the value of kingdom work. It is the most important business that has ever taken place or ever will take place on this earth. Period. And a deacon's personal walk with Christ should demonstrate his application of kingdom principles in the midst of whatever news may be coming our way—good or bad.

When we think about a deacon's *walk*, we are referring to two critical areas of his life: his *conduct* and his *conversation*. The Bible provides a clear picture in Acts 6 of a godly deacon's walk in one of the seven men selected to serve the early church—Stephen. Stephen was serious about God's business, and deacons today should be just as serious as he was.

Needless to say, Stephen certainly met all the qualifications for a deacon. The Scriptures singled him out from the other six men. Observe the following passage:

Therefore, brethren, seek out from among you seven men of good reputation, full of the Holy Spirit and wisdom, whom we may appoint over this business…and they chose Stephen, a man full of faith and the Holy Spirit… (Acts 6:3, 5)

Stephen is best remembered as the first New Testament martyr, based on Acts 7:54-60, where the details of his death are recorded, including how he responded to those who killed him. Let's read Stephen's response to the mob.

And they stoned Stephen as he was calling on God and saying, 'Lord Jesus, receive my spirit.' Then he knelt down and cried out with a loud voice, 'Lord, do not charge them with this sin.' And when he had said this, he fell asleep. (Acts 7:59-60)

It takes a godly *walk* to respond like Stephen did. A deacon who desires to live as God wants him to live should follow this biblical model. Stephen led an exemplary life which personified much of New Testament scripture. His focus on the Lord Jesus indicated in the above passage is clarified well by the Apostle Paul:

If then you were raised with Christ, seek those things which are above, where Christ is, sitting at the right hand of God. Set your mind on things above, not on things on the earth. For you died, and your life is hidden with Christ in God.

When Christ who is our life appears, then you also will appear with Him in glory. (Colossians 3:1-4)

Three characteristics of Stephen's life teach deacons how to walk in a way that fulfills the ministry for which they have been singled out.

STEPHEN'S GODLY WALK

Stephen's Walk of Fullness

The early church was grateful that God had placed men in their midst whose walk with God was characterized as *fullness.* When the church "looked out among them" (Acts 6:3), they were looking for those whose reputations had been time-tested and proven. In prayerfully thinking through the situation, the apostles identified six specific character qualifications, and Stephen met all six.

> A deacon's *conduct* and *character* ought to stand out in such a way that people both inside and outside the church count him as an honorable man.

1. Men known to be honorable – "*seek out from among you.*" The church's challenge is to choose those men who stand out because they have earned respect for the lives they live. Dependable men whom the people would be happy to follow are often the kind of men who will make good deacons. A deacon's *conduct* and *character* ought to stand out in such a way that people both inside and outside the church count him as an honorable man. God raises up in every church such men, and it is the responsibility of the church to seek them out.

2. Men who would serve with others on a team – "*seven men.*" Men on a team must be able to serve together, listen to others' opinions, put the good of others first, etc. Someone said it well: "Teamwork simply stated is less *me* and more *we.*" The seven men were a *we,* not a *me.* Deacons who focus on the will of God and the good of the church do not insist on getting their way when decisions need to be made. Instead, a good deacon insists that church work worth doing is worth doing together.

3. Men who were of *"good reputation."* Honesty and the trust of others both inside and outside the church form the foundation of a deacon's reputation. Deacons handle the church's minsitry resources and appropriately disperse them to others; therefore, deacons must be men with an impeccable reputation. A good deacon believes his reputation is worth more than gold.

4. Men filled with the Spirit of God – "*full of the Holy Spirit.*" A deacon should spend quality time alone with God reading the Bible, allowing God to mold his character; and seeking guidance, wisdom, cleansing and fresh grace to live each day. It is during this time with God that a deacon asks the Lord to fill him with the Holy Spirit, to clothe him with humility, to empower him for service, and to guard him from temptation.

The first deacons were men who, upon examination by the church, were known to be men filled with the Holy Spirit. The church should expect no less today. Every man who serves as a deacon should be full of the Holy Spirit.

5. Men who were wise and competent – "*full of wisdom.*" One scientist quipped, "Science is organized knowledge. Wisdom is organized life." A deacon with "wisdom" serves the church in a skillful, deliberate and organized way. In Stephen's day, a lack of skill would have only added to the murmuring of disgruntled church members. It is vital that we are wise in meeting the needs of the people appropriately. A wise deacon handles people and their needs with proper care, knowing that unrest and disharmony within the church quench God's glory in the church.

6. Men who were responsible and diligent – "*whom we may appoint over this business.*" Being a deacon is not about status; it is about service. It is not a position to *hold*; it is a work to *do.* In getting that work done, many churches find that in a rotating system, more men have an opportunity to serve and are thereby able to accomplish more ministry and service than in a system where deacons are appointed for life, without rotation.

Stephen's Walk of Faithfulness

Stephen's life was marked by *fullness* and *faithfulness*. Remember, it is recorded twice that Stephen was "full of faith" (Acts 6:5, 8). He was faithful to the Gospel, faithful to his testimony, and faithful to the truth of Scripture. The biblical record shows three ways faithfulness characterized Stephen's walk.

1. He was faithful with God's ministry (Acts 6:8). Notice that the passage said he "did great wonders and signs." If God has given us a ministry, then He expects us to do something with it. Stephen was faithful to carry out what God had given him and gifted him to do. Remember, deacons are given a work to do more than a position to fill.

2. He was faithful with the gospel message (Acts 6:10). Stephen knew the Bible and was a great apologist—defender of the faith. He personified it this way:

> *But sanctify the Lord God in your hearts, and always be ready to give a defense to everyone who asks you a reason for the hope that is in you, with meekness and fear.* (1 Peter 3:15)

3. He was faithful with good motives (Acts 6:15). Stephen's countenance glowed from the inside out. That's just the way it is: one's inner life cannot remain hidden. Not only must a deacon's heart be pure, but a deacon's motive must be pure and undefiled as he serves the church that ordained him.

Stephen's Walk of Forgiveness

Stephen's life was marked by fullness, faithfulness, and forgiveness. Stephen practiced the teachings of Jesus from the Sermon on the Mount about forgiveness (Matthew 5:43-46), and he practiced the principle of overcoming evil with good about which the Apostle Paul wrote (Romans 12:17-21).

Stephen's walk of forgiveness afforded him a standing ovation—"But he...saw the glory of God, and Jesus standing on the right hand of God...." (Acts 7:55). What higher honor could there be? In his forgiveness, Stephen was just like Jesus (Luke 23:34).

SUMMARY

A deacon who is going to be all God wants him to be is a deacon like Stephen. His walk will be characterized by the fullness of the Holy Spirit, faithfulness in serving both God and the church, and forgiveness in his relationships with others.

Being a deacon is not about status; it is about service. It is not a position to *hold;* it is a work to *do.*

DISCUSSION & APPLICATION

1. Discuss as a group some of the qualities you see in Stephen and jot them down in the space below. Which of these qualities do you see in yourself, and which ones do you need to see more of?

_____

_____

2. Are the deacons in your church elected to serve for life or do they serve on a rotation basis? What do you feel are the pros and cons of each method, and why has your church chosen the method it follows?

_____

_____

3. In your opinion, why is teamwork so important in deacon ministry? Why not just let each deacon serve as he feels led without concern as to what the other deacons are doing? What would you recommend doing in the case of a deacon who will not serve at all?

_____

_____

4. We identified six character qualifications of a deacon. Divide up into small groups of 2 to 4 and rank these qualifications in order of importance. Share with each other why you chose that order.

_____

_____

5. Do you feel like you are fulfilling all of the character qualifications of a deacon? If not, which one(s) do you need to work on? Develop a plan to help you become more like Stephen.

_____

_____

6. We talk about "serving God with your whole heart." What does this phrase suggest to you? With all the pressures and stresses of our culture today, do you think it is even possible for a deacon to serve with his "whole" heart? What barriers do deacons face today that deter them from serving wholeheartedly, and how can these barriers be overcome?

_____

_____

Greg is a deacon at Suburban Community Church, a church that relocated from the inner city five years ago. He is also a commercial contractor who enjoys a good reputation among Christians and non-Christians alike. He's a natural go-to kind of guy who gets things done. Recently Greg was asked by the city council to serve as chairman of a volunteer committee to oversee the construction of a new city park, complete with athletic fields and playgrounds. It's at least a 12 to 15-month project. About a week after Greg committed to the park project, the deacon officers at Suburban decided to ask him to head up a ministry team to assist senior adult members with things they can no longer do around their homes, like painting, small repairs, taking them on errands and the like. Because of his reputation for excellence and dependability—and because no one else is willing to accept the job—Greg seems to be the man to call on to coordinate this new ministry, even though the deacon officers know of his heavy commitment to the park project—not to mention the responsibility of running his own construction company.

If you were one of the deacon officers, and you were aware of Greg's willing nature toward ministry, how would you feel about asking him to head up the new ministry? Would it be wise and fair? What other options might be available? In your church, what factors do you consider when asking someone to head up a project or accept a responsibility?

_____

_____

_____

_____

PRAYER OF COMMITMENT

Heavenly Father, thank you for the example of Stephen. I pray that I would be full of faith, the Holy Spirit, and godly wisdom just like Stephen was. Help me to apply the kingdom principles so evident in Stephen's life that I might become the deacon you want me to be. Thank you, Lord, for your faithfulness and grace toward me. In Jesus' name, Amen.

DEACON MINISTRY HIGHLIGHT

NOTE: Here is a church that is recognized for having an effective deacon ministry. If time permits, review the profile below as a group, then discuss any ideas or procedures you might apply in your own deacon ministry.

FIRST BAPTIST CHURCH FESTUS/CRYSTAL CITY
107 Truman Blvd.
Crystal City, Missouri 63019
(636) 937-3668
Tim Baker, Pastor

Church & Staff

First Baptist Church Festus/Crystal City is surrounded by a well-educated, predominately Caucasian community with an almost 50% single adult population and a median household income above $50,000. In its 118-year history, FBCFCC has sponsored several mission churches and new ministries, and has been active in local and foreign missions outreach. Tim Baker has served as pastor of FBCFCC since 2006. The church has a total membership of 1,500, an average Sunday morning worship attendance of around 600, and a Sunday School attendance of around 350. In addition the pastor, the church has a full-time associate pastor, minister of music, and student minister.

Deacon Organization & Ministry

FBCFCC currently has 23 deacons who meet monthly by themselves and quarterly with the pastor and staff. The goal of the quarterly meetings is to discuss the priorities of current and future ministries, while the monthly meetings involve the planning and implementation of their responsibilities within those ministries, which include ministering to single parents, shut-ins, nursing home residents; visiting hospitals and meeting other needs within the church and the community. The deacons at FBCFCC also serve as altar counselors during the invitation time. Their goal is to lead by example.

Deacon Qualifications & Selection Process

At FBCFCC, the pastoral staff and current deacons interview potential new deacons to determine if they meet the biblical qualifications. Upon meeting those requirements and completion of a deacon covenant, through prayer and continued consideration, potential new deacons are invited into a 6-month internship where they can be mentored and observed prior to ordination. Ordained deacons maintain their office for life in an active or inactive status unless circumstances dictate otherwise.

Success Factors

The deacons at FBCFCC are developing a positive, supportive relationship with their pastor and staff, especially during the past two years while Pastor Baker has been leading them to transition from a church oversight role to a church-serving role. He applauds the deacons for their love and support and is humbled that they pray for him, seek ways to help him, and consult with him about how to serve more effectively. Being a deacon at FBCFCC is considered a great privilege because it enables each man to engage in hands-on ministry, influence the spiritual maturity of the church, and invest in people—all to the glory of God.

C H A P T E R

6

THE DEACON AND HIS WITNESS

Sharing Christ Faithfully and Helping the Church to Grow

INTRODUCTION

As a pastor, I have found that churches that enthusiastically embrace the biblical model for the office of deacon agree that there is no substitute model to be found anywhere. This model works! Now in our final lesson, we focus on the deacon's *witness*. Note the qualification the Apostle Paul writes:

> *Likewise deacons must be…holding the mystery of the faith in a pure conscience.* (1 Timothy 3:8-9)

God calls deacons to serve, and a critical part of that service is being a faithful witness for Jesus Christ. A deacon who witnesses shares what Christ has done in his own life, and how Christ can make a difference in every person's life.

Just as Stephen is a biblical model of a deacon and his faithful *walk*, Philip is a biblical model of a deacon and his faithful *witness*. Philip was one of the "seven men" chosen in Acts 6. He served the church well as a deacon, but he also became widely known as a soul-winner—an evangelist. Every time the Bible mentions Philip, he is preaching the Gospel of Jesus Christ.

> *On the next day we who were Paul's companions departed and came to Caesarea, and entered the house of Philip the evangelist, who was one of the seven, and stayed with him.* (Acts 21:8)

In Acts 8:5, the Bible shows that Philip was willing to go to people who were *different*: "Then Philip went down to the city of Samaria, and preached Christ unto them." Pride can cause a person to view those who are different as inferior and, therefore, unworthy of inclusion in the church. God loves people of all colors, races, cultures, and socio-economic status in the same way. He is no respecter of persons (Acts 10:34). Deacons must be faithful to witness to everyone, regardless of who they are or what they have.

Furthermore, the Bible shows Philip going to people who were *distant*.

> *Now an angel of the Lord spoke to Philip, saying, 'Arise and go toward the south along the road which goes down from Jerusalem to Gaza. This is desert.' So he arose and went. And behold, a man of Ethiopia, a eunuch of great authority under Candace the queen of the Ethiopians, who had charge of all her treasury, and had come to Jerusalem to worship, was returning. And sitting in his chariot, he was reading Isaiah the prophet…Then Philip opened his mouth, and beginning at this Scripture, preached Jesus to him.* (Acts 8:26-40)

God took Philip out of Samaria where revival had

broken out everywhere and sent him a great distance to save one man. This eunuch was the first recorded convert from the continent of Africa, and God used a deacon to reach him. This speaks volumes to deacons today. A deacon who is faithful in his witness should never underestimate how God might choose to use him to reach masses of people—or even a single man—with the Gospel.

> A deacon who witnesses shares what Christ has done in his own life, and how Christ can make a difference in every person's life.

In a culture that viewed women much differently from the way they are viewed today, Philip did not let gender change the simple message of the Gospel. He shared with everyone indiscriminately.

But when they believed Philip as he preached the things concerning the kingdom of God and the name of Jesus Christ, both men and women were baptized. (Acts 8:12)

Deacons should see themselves as missionaries and those they meet as a mission field. God strategically places his servants so that they can influence those around them with the Gospel of Jesus Christ. Today's church experiences much greatness—great church members, great ministries, great teachers, great preachers, great music, just to name a few. We are lacking greatness, however, in the most important area of all—evangelism!

Why do deacons sometimes become unfaithful in their witness? Consider a few possible reasons:

- Apathy
- Lack of example
- Feel untrained and inadequate
- Fear
- Too busy
- Ignorance of Scripture and how to share it effectively

Philip was a deacon who considered the Great Commission a *great privilege*. He was faithful to share the Gospel while traveling to his destination as much as when he arrived at his destination. While it is true that deacons—and all Christians, for that matter—can be effective witnesses through their *walk*, nothing takes the place of sharing Christ with *words*. We use words to teach, instruct, disciple and encourage. Philip maintained a balance. He did not just discuss evangelism with other believers; he actually did evangelism. He walked it and talked it.

LESSONS FROM PHILLIP THE SOUL-WINNER

1. Philip was a pioneer in sharing the Gospel. (Acts 8:5ff) Philip was the first to take the Gospel to non-Jewish territories. Philip was an "Acts 1:8 Christian" who took the Great Commission seriously. He is a role model encouraging others to go where God tells them to go, even if no one has gone before. Faithful men share the Gospel regardless of where the Lord directs them to go.

2. Phillip shared the Gospel in difficult places. Not every place a deacon is called to minister is an easy or comfortable place to be. Like Jesus, however, Philip preached in contemptible places. Recall when Jesus traveled to Samaria and witnessed to the "woman at the well" (John 4). She was an adulterer, an outcast, and a very confused woman. Yet upon talking to Jesus, she was saved and led a city-wide revival. A deacon must be willing to share Christ with anyone at any time.

Philip was a church leader and one of the chosen "seven." If Philip had been a prideful man, he could have considered himself too elite to go to the lowly Samaritans. But he didn't have a problem with pride. Philip never got too big to make sure the Gospel reached even the lowliest of people. Deacons should do no less.

In order to reach all people, a deacon must have a vision big enough to encompass all people. Philip had a great vision for everybody to hear the Gospel of Jesus Christ. He did not confine the

Gospel to Jews only. In his mind, the Gospel had no boundaries.

The church needs deacons today with a heart for the world who will release the Gospel and not restrict it to certain people. The church should not keep sinners out, but bring sinners in. Deacons, therefore, should not be alarmed if the greatest of sinners come into the church. Instead, they should welcome them and be passionate about sharing the Gospel with them.

3. Philip did not hesitate to obey the Lord.
(Acts 8:26-30) It is important to notice in the biblical text that while Philip was traveling southwest, the man he was destined to meet was traveling northeast. If Philip had delayed for any reason, the two might never have met. In running to meet the Ethiopian eunuch, Philip demonstrated simple obedience to the Lord and the Great Commission. There is much to be said for simple obedience. When Philip obeyed the simple *call* to go, he

heard the sinner's *cry* and took advantage of the opportunity to share the Gospel.

4. Philip used the Scripture to witness for Jesus Christ. The eunuch had the Scriptures right in front of him but could not understand them until Philip explained them to him. How inspiring it is that God can use a deacon to share the truth with a sinner who would likely never discover it on his own.

SUMMARY

Philip witnessed in his neighborhood, in his work, and as he traveled. If you as a deacon will be willing to follow his example and become faithful in your witness where you live, where you work, and where you walk, you can be a catalyst for revolutionizing your church! As a Christ-sharing, soul-winning deacon, you will be able to say, "At last, I am on my way to becoming the deacon I've always wanted to be."

Deacons should see
themselves as missionaries
and those they meet as a
mission field.

DISCUSSION & APPLICATION

1. Just how important is evangelism in the life of a deacon anyway? Is it more important for a deacon to share the Gospel than it is for any other Christian? Share your thoughts with the group.

    _____

    _____

2. Share together what it means to be an example before others of how to live for Christ. Are you as a deacon trying to fulfill this mission? How can you and others improve in this area?

    _____

    _____

3. Discuss for a few moments some of the barriers you face in boldly sharing the Gospel. Brainstorm creative ways to evangelize those around you.

    _____

    _____

4. We state in the lesson that deacons should see themselves as missionaries and everyone they meet as a mission field. Do you agree with this statement? Why or why not?

    _____

    _____

5. As a deacon, are you always aware that some of the people around you may have never heard the Gospel? Discuss possible ways to witness to people at work, in the community, and even at church. Is there a universal way to witness or must you have a different witnessing style for each situation?

    _____

    _____

6. Think about the mission field around you in light of Acts 1:8. How does the phrase "Jerusalem, Judea, Samaria, and the ends of the earth" relate to the church you serve, and are you taking the Gospel to those areas? How can your deacon body make a difference in carrying out the Great Commission?

    _____

    _____

LifeScene

Rick and his family attend a church in the metro area where he serves as a deacon. He is serious about being a deacon and is continuing to grow in his relationship with Christ. For the last few weeks, God has been dealing with Rick in his personal quiet time concerning being a bolder witness, but because he is somewhat introverted, he finds it difficult to engage in a conversation about deep spiritual matters with another person, especially if the situation is the least bit confrontational. The church Rick serves has an organized outreach program and is involved in missions overseas, but Rick has not yet felt comfortable being involved in either one. Sometimes he feels convicted to the point of stepping up and getting involved, and sometimes he feels condemned to the point of stepping down from the deacon ministry. Rick desperately wants help but is afraid to admit his fear to anyone—except to his wife, who has an outgoing personality and is a bold witness. She encourages him to share his concerns with the pastor, for whom both she and Rick have great respect.

If you were Rick's pastor, and he came to you for counsel in this matter, what would you tell him? Would you recommend that he resign from the deacon body, encourage him to channel his ministry efforts in more comfortable directions, or just tell him not to be concerned about it? After all, he's not the only deacon who doesn't witness. How would you try to help him?

_____

_____

_____

_____

PRAYER OF COMMITMENT

Father, I ask you to help me become the witness I know I should be and can be. Help me to recognize and take advantage of opportunities to share my faith with others wherever I am. Help me remember that I am called to be the light of the world, sharing the Gospel message so that people will be saved. I surrender my will to you and commit to you that I am going to be a deacon who is concerned about souls. That is the kind of deacon I am determined to be. In Jesus' name, Amen!

DEACON MINISTRY HIGHLIGHT

NOTE: *Here is a church that is recognized for having an effective deacon ministry. If time permits, review the profile below as a group, then discuss any ideas or procedures you might apply in your own deacon ministry.*

FIRST BAPTIST CHURCH WOODSTOCK

11905 Hwy 92

Woodstock, Georgia 30188

(770) 926-4428

Johnny Hunt, Pastor

Church & Staff

Enon Church relocated from 10 miles north of Canton, Georgia, to present day Woodstock in 1884, and officially changed its name to First Baptist Church Woodstock. For the next 100 years it functioned as a small community church. In 1986, FBCW called Johnny Hunt to be their pastor, and the church began to experience unprecedented growth. In 1987, the church relocated to its present 90-acre site on Hwy 92, and has continued to build facilities for worship and ministry to the culturally diverse north metro Atlanta region ever since. With over 16,000 members, FBCW averages 6,500 in worship and 5,000 in Sunday School. FBCW has 160 full-time and part-time staff members including 35 ministers who serve in pastoral care, music, education, missions, counseling, and operations. The church has sponsored nearly 100 church plants and sent out approximately 150 missionaries in the last 20 years.

Deacon Organization & Ministry

FBCW has 70 active deacons who serve for a 3-year term. Monthly deacon meetings are led by the chairman and focus on the previous month's activities, discussion of ministry needs for the coming month, followed by a time of encouragement and challenge from Pastor Johnny. The goal of the deacon ministry is to represent the pastor in visiting the sick, ministering to widows and orphans, and carrying out other assignments as directed by the pastor. The deacons at FBCW also serve as altar counselors during the invitation time of the church services, are on call every afternoon after the church switchboard closes, and are instrumental in the assimilation of new members into the church.

Deacon Qualifications & Selection Process

Deacon candidates are nominated by the church body and then interviewed by current deacons and ordained staff members to determine if they are qualified. (Divorce on the part of deacon or his spouse prevents qualification.) Qualified candidates then begin an orientation process that leads to ordination. Deacons at FBCW serve a 3-year term, after which they must rotate off for one year before serving again. Additional terms of service require the same process of nomination, interview and orientation.

Success Factors

The deacons at FBCW consider themselves servants rather than an administrative or governing body, thereby allowing them to stay on the leading edge of ministry by taking care of the needs of the church and the community as the pastor leads. The deacons meet weekly with the pastor to pray for upcoming worship services and often connect with him during the week through service and fellowship.